Alumni Anecdotes

Compiled by

Fazli Sameer

to
"All those wonderful People with whom we were raised, learned and laughed in those memorable times"

Contents

Sameer, Fazli
Alumni Anecdotes / Fazli Sameer
ISBN 9798436258966

1. People, Culture & Society, English

Alumni Anecdotes
Fazli Sameer
Colombo, Sri Lanka
fazlis@gmail.com

First Print - 2022
ISBN: 9798436258966

Published by:
Cover/Graphic Design: Fazli Sameer
Printed by : Amazon/KDP/MCR/Kobo/AJP

All Saints College

Ananda College, Colombo

Following a meeting of Buddhists at **Pettah**, under the patronage of **Hikkaduwe Sri Sumangala Thera**, an English-Buddhist school was inaugurated at 19 Prince Street on 1 November 1886 by the Buddhist Theosophical Society. The first session was attended by 37 students. In 1888, when about 130 boys were attending, it moved to 61 Maliban Street. **CW Leadbeater** was appointed the first principal of *Ananda today*.

By the time the school was officially registered in March 1889, there were 120 students. That same year, JPR Weerasuriya became the first Anandian to pass the Cambridge junior examination. The Cambridge graduate and confessed Buddhist AE Buultjens became principal.

In March 1890, the school's proximity to a Catholic school led to controversy—and a move to 54 Maliban Street where further growth ensued, and student enrolments rose to 200 in September 1892 and 270 in 1894.[1] As principals followed **Don Baron Jayatilaka**. That year, Mr Tudor Rajapaksha donated 3.2 acres (13,000 m^2) of land and the school was relocated in the suburb of **Maradana**. On 17 August 1895, the former *English Buddhist School* was renamed to *Ananda College Colombo* with **RA Mirando** serving as its manager till his death during the **1915 riots**.

When **Patrick de Silva Kularatne** took over in 1918 attendance was 450 which rapidly increased to 1000 two years later. At this time the annual budget was Rs 80,000.

By 1961, the college had officially become a government school

Ananda old boys: Sets of brothers Sunday Observer Jan 20, 2002

by B. Donald Perera

I joined Ananda College, Colombo in January 1935 and was a hosteller for 10 years. Going down memory lane I would like to reminisce on the sets of brothers who were hostellers during this period. Pride of place goes to the Herath Gunaratnes from Galmuruwa, Madampe they were Charlie, Cyril, Austin who became doctors, Lionel and Hubert.

There had been four other brothers of the same family prior to 1935. Among them one being a Buddhist priest. They had a hostel room for themselves, shared in addition by a nephew Augustus, a son of the eldest Guneratne, and a first cousin Kumarasena Wijesinghe.

Four Bodinagoda brothers, Banduwardewa during whose captaincy Ananda had won all cricket matches against all other schools in 1934, Ranapala who was Chairman Lake House, Risisoma who passed out as a doctor and went to India on a holiday during the Hindu Muslim riots, and was never heard of thereafter, the last was Leelaratne a banker popularly known as Dekka.

The Four Peiris brothers L.D.H. (David) who was later principal Royal College, Colombo, L.H.R. who was a permanent secretary of the Ministry of Justice, L.C.H. a businessman and L.R.H. Four de Silva brothers, Harry a fine athlete, Noel a journalist at Lake House, Barcroft (Barky) who was a planter, and Lloyd who was Senior Secretary in the Ministry of Transport.

Four Rajakaruna brothers from Kitulgoda, Edmund one of the fastest bowler during his time. Herbert a fine athlete, and soccer player. Austin an all-rounder, cricket, athletics and soccer and Earnest a member of the Governor's cup team in shooting.

It would not be out of place to mention here that Ananda was the only school to win this trophy and they won it twice competing with the Ceylon Planters Rifle Association (European) and the army. The four P.L. brothers from Deniyaya, PL Jinadasa was won the Deniyaya seat in 1977 but was unfortunate to sit in Parliament as he died before the first sitting, PL Chandradasa a cricketer and athlete, PL Premadasa and PL Buddhadasa.

Another unforgettable event was when Principal Mr. P. de S. Kularatne returned to Ananda in 1936 after a reorganization period at Dharmaraja College, Kandy, and temporarily occupied 3 rooms in the hostel with Mrs Hilda Kularatne, sons Ananda, Parakrama, and daughter Maya, who is now a live wire and an active member of the Senior Ananda OBA.

Three Jinadasa brothers from Bulathkohupitiya, Melville, Franklyn and Allen all of whom were well recognized planters. The Athukoralas, from Palmadulla were Cyril, later a planter, Upali a doctor, and Dhanapala (EAD) who is a retired Judge of the Supreme Court.

Three Silva brothers Ananda de Silva, later attached to the Fisheries Department, Upali a Chartered Accountant, and FAO Rome, and Nissanka an Engineer. The Karunatilaka brothers from Kalawila, Bentota, Chandrasoma, Abeysoma and Wijesoma. Fernando brothers sons of the COC bus magnate B.J. Fernando, Richard who was a superb cricketer who captained Ananda and also played for combined Colleges during his time, Sirisena, Sammy who died very young, during his school days.

The Gunasekera brothers AWS who was later Commissioner of Examinations AHS and AAH. Three Perera brothers Dannister, Neville and Granville.

SS Wijesinghe, Sam Wijesinghe who was the Director General of Parliament, and an elder brother whose initials I cannot recollect. SJP Wickramasuriya (Kolla) and younger brother who was a brilliant mathematician.

Two Samaranayaka brothers from Kumbuke, Horana, ADP and ADH. The Martin brothers Henry and Jeffry from Hatton. VK Wilbert Perera and VK Premaratna from Kegalle.

Chandrasena and brother Dayananda Fernando. Lasil and Linton Soysa from Panadura, the latter was an executive at Bartleet company, Jayaneil and Wijesoma Peiris from Panadura. K. Harischandra and K. Karunasena from Hikkaduwa both of whom were teachers.

There were also three Gunasekere brothers, sons of Mr. D.S. Gunasekere who was a Member of Parliament.

Quite a lot of the above brothers are no more, it may be that I have missed some siblings during this period as it is more than fifty seven years since my leaving school, I hope I would be forgiven by all of them.

Asoka Vidyalaya (College)

In 1971, Mr. Premadasa Udugama, the then Secretary to the Ministry of Education, had a concept to build three new Primary model schools in Colombo District. As a result Mahnama, Sirimavo & Asoka had been put forward in line with a broader perspective. Though both Sirimavo and Mahanama were granted two lands with buildings, Asoka received only a small plot of bare land at Maradana.

Those days, Maradana was yet another busiest town as today and the land was belonged to a foreigner called "Stock" and used for the collection of garbage in the surrounded areas. Not only that the area was occupied with all types of bad people. With all these factors, it was not an easy task to commence a school in the given land. At that stage, Mr. V. Weerakoon, the Education Director was searched for a talented person who could take the challenge. Finally he found a person whom he thinks fit enough to meet this challenge. He is Mr. M.P. Dharmaratne worked as an education officer in Avissawella educational division by that time. He was born in 16th August 1933 and trained as a Teacher attached to the Teacher Training Institute in Maharagama during 1953/1954. Considering all these facts Mr Dharmaratne was called upon to Colombo and he was pleased to accept the invitation of Mr Weerakoon to build up a new primary school without any hesitation. This challenge will never be accepted by anyone who knows about the surrounded environment

Bishops College, Colombo

Bishop's College is one of the oldest private Girls' Schools in Sri Lanka. The school was founded by the then Anglican Bishop of Colombo, Bishop James Chapman (1845 to 1862) and his wife Frances, originally in 1857 as a mission school for girls of elite Christian families and other European residents. After a lapse of several years the school was re-opened in 1875. It was later administered by the Sisters of St. Margaret who journeyed to Sri Lanka from East Grinstead, Sussex, United Kingdom.

The school motto, "Non Sibi Sed Omnibus" means "Not for Self but for All".

Clifton Balika MV

Clifton Balika vidyalaya is next to Maligakanda and is located in Western, Sri Lanka

Clifton provides disciplined ladies to the nation
Sunday Times Mar 2 2014

College Band at a performance initial stages the school had functioned in a Catholic background under the leadership of a great educationist, Miss Harriet Ferdinand. In 1962 the school was taken over by the Government

Clifton Girls' High school now known as Clifton Balika Maha Vidyalaya is a century old academic institution. It is not an impassive collection of buildings but a school which travels with the vision of "Providing well- disciplined ladies to the Nation". The school is situated in the heart of a once non- affluent Colombo Central. But her daughters are scattered all over the world flying high the name of their Alma-Mater in various fields of life.

Clifton Girls' High School was inaugurated in July 1887, by a Scottish Businessman Charles Bertram Brodie. The school first started in a house called "Clifton" in Dematagoda and in 1892 it was the biggest Girls school in the area. It was later moved to "Palm House", the spacious residence of the manager. Here it still stands tall though it has changed quite a lot in appearance. The Cliftonians are very lucky to have their education in a surrounding which is very historical. On one side is the "Vidyodaya Pirivena" and in front is the temple of the Venerable Anagarika Dharmapala "The Maha Bhodhi Temple". During the

CMS Ladies College

In 1900 a young Irish woman Lillian Nixon, impassioned by her belief in the need for education of women, had the courage and vision to come to a far –flung colony, Ceylon to found Ladies College at the behest of the Church Missionary Society. From humble beginnings with only two students, the school has grown to be a self-supporting day and boarding school for girls aged 3 to 18 which is recognized by the Ministry of Education as a National private fee levying institution following the national curricular

Colombo Central Hindu Maha Vidyalam

Darussalam College

281, Jumma Masjid Road, Maligawatte, Colombo 01000, Sri Lanka.

Defense Services College

The **Defense Services College** is a **National school** established on 17 January 2007 for the children of military and police personnel, within the refurbished *Rifle Barracks* building built in 1860 as part of the regimental headquarters of the **Ceylon Rifle Regiment** at Rifle Green, **Slave Island**, **Colombo** 3.

De La Salle College

De La Salle College, Colombo is the only school in **Sri Lanka** dedicated to the Patron Saint of Christian Teachers St. **John Baptist de la Salle**, founder of the congregation of **De La Salle Brothers** of the Christian Schools in **Latin**: "Fratres Scholarum Christianarum" (FSC). It was established in 1905.by the La Sallian Brothers.

Devi Balika Maha Vidyalaya

By 1950 some of the recommendations of the Kannangara report had been implemented but many believed that the opportunities for educational equality were inadequate. So the state took up the recommendation of the White Paper on education (1950), to trifurcate education at grade 8, when compulsory education ended. One of the three streams was the academic. These, in keeping with this policy, Government Girls' College, Castle Street (currently known as Devi Balika Vidyalaya) was set up with classes from grade 9 to 12, catering to academically gifted girls. The Department of Education further intended this new school to be a center of excellence in science education, an area of knowledge for which there was great demand after World War II. But not long after, it became clear that trifurcation of education was not the answer to our problems. But by then the vision for Devi as a school for academically gifted girls, specially strong in science, had taken hold.

In establishing this Government Girls' College, the guidance and support received from late Mr. TD Jayasuriya as the Director of Education was admirable. This prestigious educational institution – Government Girls' College was founded on the 15th January, 1953, at Castle Street, Borella, constructed with pre fabricated material, with 53 students and 5 teachers. From the very beginning the importance of extra curricular activities was recognized though the emphasis was on academic pursuits. Girl Guiding, dancing (Kandyan, Indian and country dancing), music, sports and drama were introduced at the inception itself where by the hidden talents of many a students were discovered and channeled towards personality building.

Mrs Wimala de Silva (Late Deshabandu Dr. (Mrs) Wimala de Silva) was its founder principal. With the enthusiasm of a young and energetic staff and above all with the unstinting help of her husband - Dr. S.L. de Silva particularly in developing science teaching, she started this great voyage.

More than half a century has elapsed. Sri Lanka has been gifted with thousands of patriotic, talented and skilled daughters dedicated to duty and service to their motherland, who brought fame to their school in return.

In 1873 "the want of a 'Superior' school in connection with the Wesleyan misson work was urged by Revd Samuel Langdon and it was unanimously agreed that a Day and Boarding school should be commenced at Katukelle"

The school was opened in May 1879 at the Wesleyan School Chapel adjoining the Girls' Boarding School, Katukelle, under the management of Miss. Payne, the next Principal arrived in Colombo on 31th July 1879 but left the school in February 1880. In May 1880 Miss Hay came from England and the school which had a 10 on roll at its inception increased to 70 and was registered to obtain a grant-in-aid from the government.

As numbers increased in 1881 the school shifted to the more commodious precincts of the Mission in Brownrigg Street, but boarders remained at Katukelle. Classes were held in a hall behind the church. Heavy pews from the church were moved weekly when classes had to take their turn in writing.

Dudley Senanayake Vidyalaya

Dudley Senanayake College is situated in Park Road Close to Anderson Flats (**Colombo** 05, **Sri Lanka**). The school has nearly 2000 students. This school is popular for sports like **cricket** and **rugby**. It has a long history as a school but still lacks popularity around Sri Lanka.

In its 39-year history it has produced many graduates including doctors, engineers chemists, teachers and much more. Until the year 2000 it didn't have A/L classes. First A/L batch faced its exam in the year 2000 in Arts steam. All above mentioned science graduates are the students of

Dudley Senanayake College until their O/L. Since there was no science A/L they are compelled to go to some other school.

Dudley Senanayake Vidyalaya had a wonderful primary section during latter part of 80s to 2000. It produced many scholars which later became very bright and brilliant students of popular schools of Sri Lankan. This process hid the name of the school and illuminated the names of other schools further.

Fathima Muslim Ladies College (BV)

Founded in 1918 and is located at 155, Bandaranaika Mawatte, col-12, Colombo,

Good Shepherd Convent

On 15th April, 1869, Rev. Sr. Mary Anucita Marandi, Sr. Mary Suzanne Cardiff, Sr. Euphstie Joseph and Sr. Mary Sacred Heart Masi arrived in Sri Lanka consequent to a request made in 1867 by the then Bishop of Colombo, His Lordship Hilarion Sillani to Mother Mary of St. Euphrasia Pelletier (now St. Mary Euphrasia), to set up a school of the Good Shepherd order. The Rev. Sisters had been given a grand welcome which was followed by a Thanksgiving service.

On 1st May 1869, the school began functioning with just 8 students and the first Superior of the Convent, Sr. Mary of the Seven Dolours Joly taking over the task of leading the School as Principal.

One of the priorities of the Good Shepherd Sisters had been to pursue the construction of a Chapel. Consequently the site was blessed on 21st June 1869 and the construction was left in the able and artistic hands of Fr. Stanislaus Tabarrani, who was then regarded as a world icon in par with popular characters such as Michael Angelo. During the 1870s' the school had around 100 day scholars. The construction of a two-storey building, to house an orphanage began on 21st June 1869, guided by Bishop Sillani.

Gothami Balika Vidyalaya

The idea of establishing a government girls' school had been taken by **CWW Kannangara** at the stage of 1946, when there was no girls' school in Sri Lanka. According to that the school he started as Royal Girls' School was changed as the Government English Girls' School. Students were admitted for the new school on 10th of June in 1946. The school was started with a principal, 3 teachers and 15 students. Mrs Gladis Perera was the principal and Mrs Sheila Perera was the Deputy Principal. At the inception boys students were also admitted to the school. Norbert Perera who was the son of Mrs Gladis Perera, the principal of this school got the opportunity to enter the 1st Government English School. Sri Chandra D Abrew Wijesinghe was the student who entered to the school as the 2nd student.

Up to grade 5, the education was given in native language and above that education was given in English Medium.

At the early stage there wasn't a uniform for the school. Most of the students came to the school wearing various colors of dresses without shoes. After the uniform with the strap was started and green tie was designed to wear with that uniform. There were two gold and black strips at the bottom of the tie. According to that black, green & gold were the school colors.

In 1947 Mrs Carmon was the sports teacher in the school. Under her guidance all the students were divided into 4 houses. The four houses were **Saranath, Ajantha, Sanchi** and **Thakshila.** After that the 1st sports meet of the Government English Girls' School was held at the Campbell Place Grounds on 27 July in 1948. The 1st Prize Giving was held in December of 1995.

In 1956 Mrs Gladys Perera had to leave the school after finishing her service period as the principal. In this period the medium of teaching was changed to Sinhala after Mrs Soma Premaratna appointed as the principal. As a result of this the Government English Girls' School was named as Gothami Balika Vidyalaya.

At that time the school uniform was also changed. Instead of the girls uniform with colours, the uniform with square neck and 4 fleets was introduced.

The school anthem was created by Mrs Hema Malini, the teacher who was in staff of the school. In 1993 the Gothami Balika Vidyalaya became as a National School

Hameed Al Husseini College

It is no exaggeration to say that the history of the early beginnings of Hameed Al Husseinie Maha Vidyalaya is the history of the efforts of Muslim leaders to set up educational institutions of their own for the children of their community. This was a problem faced by Buddhists and Hindus too: they did not want their children to be taught in an atmosphere hostile to indigenous culture and tradition and above all their religions. They found a satisfactory solution under the leadership of Col. Olcott and Arumuga Navalar by establishing educational institutions for Buddhist and Hindu establishment of the Aligarh Movement by Sir Essayed Ashamed Khan.

At this period of crisis for Muslim of Ceylon Mohamed Cassim Siddi Lebbe appeared as a Proctor in Kandy.

He urged his fellow men to expand the horizon of education, then confined only to Qur'anic studies and other allied Islamic subjects. His fight was against heavy odds; the Muslim were suspicious of the motives of the British opening schools for the spread of English education. This was not without foundation for the official patronage given to Christian Mission Schools and the passing of certain legislation led to confusion of beliefs and decay of traditional customs.

However, Siddi Lebbe's efforts were not to be frustrated; he enlisted the help of Orabi Pasha, the Egyptian exile and Wapche Marikar, one of the most trusted and respected leaders of the Muslims of Colombo, for the promotion of education.

With the inauguration of the Anglo-Mohamedan School on 15th November, 1884 in the school in New Moor Street, Colombo, dawned a new epoch for Muslim education and social awareness. Siddi Lebbe, in his speech at the inauguration ceremony, explained the objectives and made a fervent plea for funds to meet the cost for the maintenance of the institution, which was named Al Madrasathul Khairiyathul Islamia in deference to the wishes of Orabi Pasha.

This appeal met with a property worth Wapche Marikar leading the rest with a magnificent gift of a property worth Rs.3000/=, a princely sum then, and Orabi Pasha making his own contribution of Rs.100/= out of his meager allowance.

In a stirring speech, charged with emotion. Orabi Pasha appealed to all Muslim to unite forgetting their petty differences. He quoted copiously from Al Quran and Hadith on the duties of Muslims, their relations with one another and the noble heritage of the Prophet of Allah and his companions, to which they were heir. They were heir. This speech produced an astounding effect on the audience. The people were moved to tears; the leaders of various factions among the Muslims who had resorted to litigation over trivial matter, realizing their folly, sought immediate reconciliation, offering salaams, embracing one another. Thus, the inauguration ceremony of the school did create something short of a social revolution among the Muslims and produced a climate in which educational backwardness was to be removed.

Hindu College

The College started as a Pillayaar School on 12 Feb 1951 by The Hindu Educational Society, Colombo with 55 students and 2 teachers. It has now grown to over 4,000

students and 250 teachers and is regarded as one of the leading government national schools in the country. The first principal of this school was Mr Pathmanathan.

The school has four main houses namely; Kambar, Valluvar, Barathi and Illango (the four most important historians in Tamil language history) which are used to represent the students at the Sports meet which is held annually. The school anthem was written in 1976 mentioning these four houses very often in the anthem.

Holy Family Convent, Bambalapitiya

Holy Family Convent, Bambalapitiya was founded in the year 1903 by the Sisters of the Holy Family Congregation of Bordeaux. The school, which started with a small group of students and few nuns, has developed magnificently achieving excellence, and shines radiating love amidst the vim, vigor and vitality of youth. Throughout 118 long years the Holy Family Congregation has succeeded in maintaining the ideals of the Holy Family of Nazareth, mainly due to their dedication, adaptability and infinite faith in Divine Providence."

Isipathana College

In January 1952, with an intake of 400 boys, who constituted the overflow from the **Royal Preparatory School**, Greenlands College was established in a coconut grove amidst **Havelock Town** on Greenlands Road (after which it was named), about 7 acres (28,000 m^2) in extent.[

The first principal was B A Kuruppu (1952-1959) who was then the vice-principal of Blue Street Central College, **Kotahena**.

The initial admissions were made by a Board composed of principals of **Royal College Colombo** and **Thurstan Colleges** and the headmaster of Royal Preparatory School; classes were organised in all three streams - **Sinhala**, **Tamil** and English, with a tutorial staff of seven teachers.

The college crest was designed by the first principal with the assistance of J. D. A. Perera and Stanley Abeysinghe of Heywood School of Art, it consists of a lighted lamp and an opened book with the motto "Strive with determination" below. The college colours are dark and light green which was selected from the name of the college (Greenland College).

The first sports meet was held in March 1953 and the first prize-giving in 1954.

The first issue of the college magazine came out in 1954. In 1956 Vihara Mandiraya and Chaitya were built to commemorate "Buddha Jayanthi year" at school premises. The college had adapted itself to the socio-cultural changes which were taking place since Buddha Jayanthi in 1956 which led to the renaming of the college in 1961. Greenlands Road had been renamed as Isipathana Mawatha[4] after **Isipathanaramaya Temple** and the school was renamed as Isipathana Maha Vidyalaya. Within a decade Greenlands became Isipathana.

In 1962, the college was divided into two schools as Kanishta (junior) and Jeshta (upper) Vidyalayas (colleges) with two separate principals. In 1975 the Education Department amalgamated Kanishta Vidyalaya (junior college) with the Maha Vidyalaya (senior college).[citation needed]

In 1999 the schools were amalgamated into a single college under one principal.

The school currently has more than 5,000 students enrolled, from grades 1 to 13.

The school anthem is "Sarade Matha Isipathanaya apa..."

CWW Kannangara College

Dr. Christopher William Wijekoon Kannanga; 13 October 1884 – 23 September 1969) was a Sri Lankan lawyer and a politician. Rising up the ranks of Sri Lanka's movement for independence in the early part of the 20th century, he became the first Minister of Education in the State Council of Ceylon, and was instrumental in introducing extensive reforms to the country's education system that opened up education to children from all levels of society.

Born in the Southern coastal town of Hikkaduwa, his academic prowess enabled him to win a Foundation Scholarship to Richmond College, Galle, a prestigious secondary school at the time. After leaving school, he worked as a teacher in Mathematics at Wesley College, Colombo and Prince of Wales College, Moratuwa. He excelled as a lawyer in the Southern Province which made the public of the area to nominate him to contest at the legislative council election representing the Southern Province at which he made an easy win as a member of the legislative council. This was the beginning of his political career. Later, he entered the national movement for independence. Kannangara was first elected to the Ceylon Legislative Council in 1923 and then to the State Council. He also served as the President of the Ceylon National Congress.

Khairiya Islamic Balika Vidyalaya

Established in 1878

Lindsay Girls School (BV)

" Far around the world thy children sing their song
From East and West their voices sweetly blend
Praising the Lord in whom young lives are strong…."

These opening lines of the original school hymn spells out the vision of the founders a century ago, when at 1030 hrs on Monday 03rd September 1900, Bambalapitiya Girls'

High School came into being.

Founded by the Dutch Reform Church to serve the girls living in and around Bambalapitiya, the school was renamed Lindsay Girls' School after Rev. Lindsay the priest in charge of the Bambalapitiya parish. Twenty nine pupils, three teachers – Mrs Grace Ebert, May Foenander and Florence Fruitner, the Principal – Mrs Paulusz and the manger Rev. Tweed created history by being the first to be associated with the new institution.

The development of the school can be considered in two stages. 1900 – 1962 and the other stage 1962 to present day. Stage one (1900 – 1962) was a period of slow but definite growth. The pioneers were faced with many constraints. The major ones were the lack of space; funds to expand and lack of support from those whom they set out to serve. The school did not have the same appeal as the larger school in Colombo. The school accommodated eight classes in one hall.

During the principal-ship of Mrs A W Felsinger (1900 - 1931) the foundation was laid for Lindsay to take her place among the girls school of today. By 1925 three new buildings were constructed with the help of fund raising exercises and a room was temporarily rented out to house the Kindergarten classes in Glen Aber Place.

Students were presented for the local elementary school leaving certificate and the Cambridge junior and senior examinations. Classes were conducted in the English medium. In 1915 a school uniform and a tie was introduced with the school colours purple and mauve. The school emblem took the form of the shield with its inspiring motto "Onward and Upward". The house system was introduced in 1931 and was named after three managers Revs. Lindsay, Tweed and Fleming. The girls guide movement was begun, by 1931 the students from the KG to the senior forms totalled to hundred.

Mrs E M Metzeling took over as principal from 1931, and till 1946 with a short break steered the destiny of the school. The past pupils' association was formed on the 08th of March 1932. By 1939 the school had a well equipped kitchen, a sick room and library. In 1941 the 'Mance' belonging to the church was made available to the school, first on a nominal rent and later free of charge. This provided more space for classrooms and by 1945 the school housed a hostel and Montessori class. With the educational reforms of 1945 Sinhala medium classes was introduced with Mrs Rajapathirana in charge. The annual sports meet was held on the school grounds and in spite of limitations Lindsay produced athletes of the calibre of June De Kretser who achieved national standards.

Under the principal-ship of Ms M.E Vandriesen's (1947 – 1961) the school further expanded by converting the existing single story building into a two storied one. In 1956 the largest of the new rooms was made the Tweed memorial library. Due to lack of space the library was converted in to classrooms in later year.

Apart from the importance given to academic studies during her period Ms Vandriesen also recognized the students love for music, song and dance. Aesthetic studies were introduced in to the school curriculum to nurture the inborn talents of the students. Elocution was tutored under Mrs Wendy Whatmore, drill and rhythmic dancing was instructed by Ms Sheila and singing was coached under Ms Olive Rode and to day continues in the school curriculum. The students of Lindsay Girls' School participated with success in inter-school drill displays, country dancing competitions, and junior and senior choral speaking choirs were presented annually for the trinity college of music for examinations. Programs of music, verse and songs were presented over the radio. The school also took part in inter-school drama competitions such as the Shakespeare drama competition organized by the thespians. Plays such as "Sophro the Wise" and "Zuraika" was staged. The literary, music and dramatic society was inaugurated on the 02nd July 1948. Lindsay Girls' School having earned a name for the high standard of music, dance and song over the years was nominated to be a centre for "Aesthetic Studies – Western" in the early 1980's.

The school also boasts of a rich history in sports. The school netball team competed with bigger schools in Colombo to win the Westrop challenge cup. Athletes were presented for the A.A.A. public school each year. The calendar of the school events was complete with the annual sports meet, prize giving, anniversary service, carol service, annual executions and inter-house netball matches. A school magazine was published annually.

Lindsay contrary to begin a girl's school has the privilege to count amongst her past pupils old boys too. The boys gained admission in 1950 and studied up to standard four. The boys having learnt their first lessons at Lindsay distinguished themselves in various spheres in Sri Lanka and overseas. Mr Richard Matzeling, Mr Desmond Fernando, Mr Peter Wille, Mr Jeff Wijesinghe, Mr Brian de Liveira and Mr Brian de Kretser are but a few such 'old boys' of the school.

Stage two (1962 to present day) of the school began with the takeover of school by the then ruling Government. With the takeover, the school was re-named as "Lindsay Balika Vidyalaya". The hostel and the Montessori classes were terminated. There were a number of principals at the helm for short periods who contributed to the school's "Onward" march with the help of the "Parents Teachers Association" which was formed in 1962, later named the "School Development Society".

The first principal to face the challenges of the takeover was Mrs C Felsianes. There grew a demand for admission to the school and to serve the increasing numbers in students on roll, the staff too expanded. Lindsay had to now cater to all sections of society. Along with the students' Christian movement and the YWCA which were in existence, Mrs Felsianes initiated the formation of the Buddhist and Islamic associations. In addition to the English drama and singing competitions which were held annually Mrs Felsianes also introduced inter-house Sinhala and Kavi (poetry) competitions.

New classrooms were built during the time of Ms A W Jayasekera, Mrs AGEP Perera and Mrs Leela Gunasinghe to cope with the increasing number of admissions to the school. 1972 saw the termination of the Samayawardene School which was located in School Lane, Kollupitiya. This building was given for the use of Lindsay. It housed three classrooms.

Further changes were brought about to the school culture. The emblem was changed to a lamp, and 4 new houses replaced the existing three and were named Shantha, Saumya, Ramya and Vinitha. A new school song was composed. G.C.E. advanced level classes (arts and commerce) were introduced under Mrs Leela Gunasinghe. Sports such as hockey were also introduced.

Credit is due to the large number of teachers who taught at Lindsay over the years. To quote Mrs Metzeling a former principal. The sentiment expressed by her is applicable to Lindsay over the years. "that the school went forward during the period was due entirely to the whole hearted sacrificing of the teachers who not only carried the burden of combined classes in many cases, but cheerfully gave of their time and strength to build the school in every possible way".

Today there are over 1500 student on roll under the guidance of their Principal Mrs Dharmadasa from its modest beginning in 1900. Lindsay has grown in every sense of the word. Past pupils of Lindsay are found all over the world. The 25th Anniversary of the Past Pupils Association of Lindsay in Australia was celebrated in April 2000.

In conclusion given below is a quote from a report made in 1948 by Ms ME Vanden Dreisen, principal, which even sums up Lindsay's role in society today:

"The difficulties of today loom large but when seen in the correct respective they will dwindle down to their correct size. In this small world of our school, we strive to set before our girls the ideals of honesty, courage and justice and aim to send out into the service of their country women who will face life with courage, kindliness and faith."

Lumbini College

Developing Lumbini College through 7 phases of Online Education, with a great commitment and enthusiasm, made Lumbini a center of education not only for our school but for any child in Sri Lankan school system. The school teachers, non-academic staff, parents and children who working hard during the Covid-19 pandemic is a well-known fact for this.

First Stage: Started from March 2020 (8.00 am to 4.00 pm) all grades from grade 1 to grade 13 were taught using social media such as sms, whatsapp, telegram viber, fb etc.

Second Stage: Initiation of Zoom, Google meeting as Online Education tools for GCE (O / L) 10,11 and GCE (A / L) 12,13.

Third Stage: Launch of a YouTube channel, FB page and a web page for the education of the children.

Fourth Stage: Under the theme 'Education for all', provide education to all children by sending hard copies to the children who do not have online facilities by contacting the parents of the class

Fifth Stage: When the country is partially open, teaching time were scheduled as below with the theme "Let's learn with parents!" due to the absence of parents at home during the day. Grades 1-5 from 6.00pm-9.00pm, grades 6-11 from 6.00pm-11.00 pm and grades 12-13 from 5.00pm to 11.00pm

Sixth Stage: Developing and implementing a system for supervising and regulating, formalizing the method of providing online link by verifying the identity of students.

Seventh Stage: Teachers were empowered to conduct online tests, online forms were prepared accordingly, and for the first time in Sri Lanka, all activities such as online examinations, online paper marking, online marks uploading were conducted before 31st December 2020.

In addition on facilitating poor children, facilitating teachers and activating smart classrooms, we also organized AL technology online practicals, online practical in aesthetic subjects and also children's programs for Vesak, Poson, Christmas day, school day and even competitions. We are happy with the children.

Mahabodhi Maha Vidyalaya

One of the leading schools in the heart of Colombo city with a diverse population of students. Mahabodhi College has held a name for a very long time in all aspects of the education, sports extra curricular activities and etc in the country. At current state, the school is being re-developed to return to its former glory.

Mahanama College

Mahanama College was founded in 1954 by W. A. K. Gunawardana in Sri Wardanarama, Colombo, with just five students in the class. In 1958, the school was registered as a government-assisted junior school. The number of students gradually increased to 163 with four staff members and, on 1 January 1960, J. D. A. Jayakodi was appointed as the first principal of the school. By 1969, there were 14 staff members and 373 students.

With the rapid increase in student enrolment, the school moved to a nearby location, Valukarama. Primary classes were held in a nearby building, **Thurstan College**. In 1974, during T. N. Silva's time as principal, the junior school at Thurstan College moved to its present location, Mahanama College. In 1975, 130 students sat for the national **General Certificate of Education**, and 107 students passed the exam. The government donated 7 acres (28,000 m^2) of land as the school expanded. By 1976, the site contained several two-story buildings.

During the early 1970s, principal N. E. Fernando made improvements to the school's facilities, including the construction of a dental unit and additional classrooms, as well as the first two-story building. Principal K. N. P. de Silva retired on 5 February 1986 and was succeeded by **DG Sumanasekera**. Sumanasekera was the first SLEAS Class-1 principal to head Mahanama. During his four years in office, he laid the foundation for the present school.

KK Rathnadasa became principal in 1990 and, during his time at the college, several three-storey buildings were constructed, a computer section was established, and a children's park was created. The annual carnival 'Foot-Loose' was also organised during his tenure.

In 1999, G Liyanage became principal. He added a three-storey building with an art gallery to the existing campus. During his tenure, the school laboratories and computer sections were improved and buildings renovated. The Battle of the Gold's also known as "Big Match" between Mahanama College and its friendly rival **DS Senanayake College**, Colombo, was inaugurated

Methodist College

Methodist College, founded in 1866 is a leading girls school in Colombo, managed by the Methodist Church in Sri Lanka. The school currently maintains a student body of 1800 and approximately 75 teachers. The institution conducts 2 streams of classes in Sinhala and Tamil with English as a second language.

Kollupitiya, one hundred and fifty years ago, was not the residential area it is today, with broad tree-lined avenues and, the wide Galle Road running along the sea front. Kollupitiya was a village with narrow tracks, cinnamon gardens and a sparse population. It had a market place with bullock carts, horse-drawn carriage and rickshaws on its roads. It was in this village, the Methodist Mission started a Sinhala School in the early part of the 19th century.

In 1866 a devout Missionary, Miss. Catherine Scott came out to Ceylon and started the Kollupitiya Girl's English School in a large room on this same spot with merely forty girls. The large room was divided into three sections – two for the Sinhala and English classes and the third for the persevering Methodist Missionary, busy learning Sinhala from a Pundit. There were no beautiful classrooms with educational aids and apparatus. By the time Ms. Scott left in 1883, the school was registered as a 'Grant-in-Aid' English High School with 99 pupils and renamed Kollupitya Girls High School. With the same determination of spirit which enabled her to last 17 years in this country, she laid the foundation for this most Christian and outstanding educational institution.

This then was the beginning of Methodist College Colombo which today is a leading secondary collegiate school for girls with classes up to the University Entrance level. It now has a manageable student body of 1800 and a staff of 76 teachers. From these meager beginnings, the school has blossomed into an outstanding multi-ethnic, multi-religious educational institution conducting classes in all 3 streams, Sinhala, Tamil, and English.

When Ms. Choate first arrived, the school compound was quite different to what it is now. It had rather a quaint layout then with the old church, the rambling mission house, Boy school, a printing office, a well with brackish water used by the printing office and a bell with a roof over it, all of which do not exist today — old fashioned landmarks now vanished forever.

Almost immediately after her arrival in 1913, Ms. Park was responsible for introducing the teaching of elementary science, a step that had far-reaching consequences for the institution. Impressive innovations followed. The First Colombo Guide Company was founded in 1917 by Ms. Choate and captained by Ms. Shire. In 1919 the Old Girls Association was established and this organization was developed into one that has ever since taken a keen and devoted interest in the welfare of the school. The MC OGA now has branches in London, Melbourne, Sydney, Toronto, Victoria, and Southern California. It has played a prominent role in fundraising for the new buildings which now grace the compound.

From the Rev. Rigby came the inspiration for the first re-building program. It was mainly due to his endeavors that some of the old buildings were pulled down or adapted and the Rigby hall completed in 1916, along with a new set of classrooms. The building of a new Hostel was a dream begun by him.

His successor, the Rev Restarick continued in his predecessor's path and gave great encouragement to the building of the new Hostel which was finally finished and opened in 1922. 1944 was another landmark when the first Sri Lankan Mrs L. G. Loos, an old girl whose father was a Methodist Minister, became Principal, succeeding Miss. Park. In 1951 M.C entered the Free Education scheme as an assisted school. In this year the College was raised to A-grade status and Miss Grace Robins took over as Principal on the retirement of Mrs Loos. These were years of further expansion and around this time Framjee House on Station Road was bought.

The new Science Block was opened in this period, and the Loos Building which has 10 classrooms was completed in 1977. It is a tribute to the Education Society, OGA, the PTA, Staff, and Pupils that this massive task was completed. With the shifting of classrooms to the new building, it was possible to provide the boarders with a reading room and library and en extra staff room. The Auditorium was declared open on June 24, 1988, by the

Rev. Harold Fernando, President of the Methodist Conference.

Thus the wheel has now completed the full circle, and from its small beginnings, it has succeeded in emerging self-sufficient, proud of its achievements – yet, with enlightenment and humility – as one of the pre-eminent schools in the country.

Muslim Ladies College

Muslim Ladies' College is known and recognized in Sri Lanka as the premier state educational institution for Muslim Girls. It is located at No 22, Kensington Garden, Colombo 00040.

When The Second World War Broke Out School Was Closed Down and the Military Has Acquired the Building. The Ceylon Moor Ladies' Union found a generous benefactor, who is none other than Sir Razik Fareed who was philanthropic to donate his land and a few buildings at fareed place to reopen the school. The school was officially reopened on the 1st of November 1946 by Honourable Minister of Education, late Mr. CWW

Kannangara. The Ceylon Moor Ladies' Union Education Committee appointed Mrs Ayesha Rauff as the Principal of MLC. Mrs Nafia Mohideen was appointed as the Manageress.

The school started with 26 students and 3 teachers but within 2 months the student population sprang up to 200 showing rapid progress. Ms Milwaganam, Ms Workmister and Mrs Nagendra were the pioneer teachers of MLC.

In 1947 a male Board of Advisors was appointed to advice on all financial matters pertaining to the management of the college.

Since then under the leadership of many graded principals the school has achieved its renown status with remarkable achievement in its academic and extra-curricular performance.

The present principal of the school Mrs MNF Nasriya assumed duties at the school on a directive issued by the secretary of Ministry of Education in 2018 and taking all her initiative to reach the excellence of our alma mater. Her vision of reach the academic excellence with the total development of student has been embedded in the school community with all the motivation.

At present the school has a student body of about 3500 and 150 teachers serving the school utmost devotion. The school serves the community from grade 1-13 in all three media where all students are offered in all four streams of studies, Arts, commerce, science and vocational streams.

Nalanda College

It was a time when the English rulers kept Buddhists under colonial heel. A time when Buddhist parents were compelled to send their children to missionary schools since there were no indigenous schools of their own. It is in this context that foreigners like Sir Henry Steel Olcott, Madame Blavatsky and Miss. Marie Musaeus Higgins arrived in this country, to help the few Buddhist leaders in their quest for moral and philosophical freedom.

When Ananda College was established in 1886, it attracted the attention of many Buddhists. Thus in no time students were drawn in from all corners of the island, craving for education catered to suit their own culture. As a result by the end of 1923, it was quite conspicuous that the infrastructure that was present could no longer cope, with the ever-increasing demand.

At that time the Ananda playground was located in Campbell Place, Colombo. Next to the playground was a stretch of land about one acre in extent. Mr P de S Kularathne the then principal of Ananda College leased this land and moved in some junior classes of Ananda. These first classrooms were simply mud huts!

This new wing of Ananda was under the authority of Mr. EW Perera. He was a very efficient administrator, who did an excellent job in keeping the place clean and maintaining discipline among students. He was well rewarded for his hard work when this new institution was readily approved by the then director of education Mr Robinson, who quite clearly was very impressed with the way it was functioning.

Mr Kularathne went even further and bought another 4 acres, from an adjacent land, which cost him 55 000 rupees at that time. A new building consisting of 16 rooms was constructed on this newly acquired land soon after. Sir Gregory Thompson, the then Governor of Ceylon, laid the foundation stone in 1922. Out of its 16 rooms, which were the best that had been built for Ananda so far, 2 were used as laboratories and 2 others as the staff room and the principal's office. The remaining 12 rooms were used as classrooms under the authority of Mr. L. H. Meththananda. Mr. E. W. Perera was appointed the head master. The Ven. Balangoda Ananda Maithriya Thero became the first Dharmarcharya.

Rathnavalie Balika Vidyalaya, Gampaha

Since 1947

Rathnavali Balika Vidyalaya is an outstanding and academically discerning girls' Buddhist high school located in Gampaha, Sri Lanka, with a well-respected history of providing excellent educational outcomes for gifted and talented young women since 1947.

The school supports the selected, fortunate young individuals in our school for their wellbeing by providing the ideal atmosphere that allows every student to thrive as they work towards achieving their best personal performance. Moreover, we set high expectations for girls and work hard to safeguard positive emotions across the school community, seeking to deepen knowledge, provide enriching and innovative learning experiences, while also softly urging the girls out of their comfort zone to attempt new challenges of the globalized world.

The school is blessed by an academic staff of 3 deputy principals, and an assistant principal and teachers those who readily inspire the students to develop creativity, confidence and resilience to become independent and ethical global citizens.

Richmond College, Galle

Among the most important business transacted at the meeting of the Missionaries of South Ceylon in the early months of 1876 in Colombo, was the recent development of the work in Galle. Owing to zealous and preserving applications of Mr. Baugh the authorities in England had decided on the establishment of a Superior School for Boys at Galle under the charge of Missionary and had made a liberal grant for erection of buildings at Richmond Hill. This District Meeting of Missionaries voted their thanks to the Committee for the generous aid and their congratulations to Mr Baugh on the success of his plans. The meeting also appointed the Rev Samuel Langdon Principal of the new school.

Work in connection with the new school in Galle progressed with feverish haste. There existed already on Richmond Hill the Boys Anglo Vernacular School. An additional building was erected where the main block of class rooms built by Mr Darrel now stands. A new bungalow close to the rooms of the Theological students was built for Mr Langdon.

Mr Baugh continued to occupy what has been since the time of Mr Darrel The Principals bungalow. Furniture was hurriedly procured, and a syllabus drawn up . When this was over the following advertisement appeared in the local papers.

Royal College, Colombo

Since 1835, Royal College has been devoted to producing gentlemen capable of spearheading change and advancement. Its multicultural environment fosters the free exchange of ideas and the celebration of diverse identities. Possessing a rich history of tradition but never limited by it, the College has always maintained adaptation as the key to excellence. From its inception at the verandah of a modest church with a mere 20 pupils to becoming the largest and most prominent educational institution in Sri Lanka, the Royal College has a documented history of nearly two centuries and counting.

Class teachers in the 50s/60s formative grade included, **Capt. MKJ Cantlay**, (later Brevet Lieut-Col. MKJ Cantlay, e.d., JP) affectionately called Canto, (1A), Messers **V Sivalingam, MM Alavi, Lieut RIT Alles** (Rita), **Abdeen, Justin de Silva**, and of course, the Headmaster of the Junior School, **Major CP de A Abeysinghe** (CowPox).

The principal of the Senior School, in the 60s, was **Mr Dudley KG de Silva**, a man of great personality, stature, discipline, and well earned respect, whose dedication and commitment to Royal, and to us, is etched in our memory palaces, and, which loyalty we shall never forget.

It would be failing not to mention two significant personalities of that era, **Mr Bogoda Premaratne** (Vice Principal) and Mr EC Gunasekara (Kataya) whose impact on all our lives is something one cannot equate materially. No doubt all the other members of the teaching and administrative staff played an important role in our lives at some stage or another during those wonderful years at Royal.

Other names of those eminent mentors who nurtured us through our academics at Royal College are Messrs **E St Elmo de Bruin** (Bruno), **Viji Weerasinghe** (Duckie), **M Ratnayake** (Ghandi), math guru **V Arasaratnam,**
S Gulasekaram (Thosay), **Hari C Arulanandan, MT Thambapillai** (Thamba), **M Muttiah, R Rajendran, V Shanmugaratnam, V Menon** (Pope), **D Weerasingham** (Blackie), **S Sabaratnam** (Half Soda), (Kota) **Silva, Sheriffdeen** (Woodwork shop), **Attanayake, Sawaad, EW Rupesinghe** (Rupperty), **Devapriya, EFC Perera, Mrs Samarasekera** (Madam), **"Teddy Bear"** of the Metal Work shop, (Kos) **Dias, John Henri de Saram,** Major **R Ratnathickam** (Rat), **A Canagaratne, Thavaneetharajah** (Thavam), **Karunaratne,** Civics guru who helped many a leading lawyer today on his career path to fame, **Thillainathan** (Liston), **VH Nanayakkara** (Nana), and **WT Canegaratnam**.

Saiva Mangayar Vidyalam (Hindu Ladies College)

Saiva Mangaiyar Vidyalayam was founded in Sept. 1932. The school commenced its sessions with only seven pupils on roll with Mrs Sivanandam Tambiyah as its first manager and Mrs Sornacanthy Nallainathan as its first headmistress.

Ms. Jeganayaki Ponniah, Ms. Leela Ponniah and Mrs Padmavathi Nagaretnam who were on the Kalagam Committee served as honorary teachers.

In 1935, the Vidyalayam was qualified to receive grant and became a Grant in Aid Education. In 1936, Ms. Kasippillai was appointed as the first principal of the Vidyalayam who guided the destiny of the school for the period of 33 years.

Seevali MMV

Sirimavo Bandaranaike Vidyalaya

Sirimavo Bandaranaike Vidyalaya was inaugurated on 1 January 1973, as Stanmore Crescent Primary School with 5 teachers and 149 students under the able guidance of Miss Wimala Liyanage, the founder principal. Her name was "Stanmore Crescent Primary School". The school consisted of classes up to grade five.

After eleven months of deliberation, the then Deputy Minister of Education **BY Tudawe** suggested to change the name of the school in honor of late Madame Sirimavo Bandaranaike who was the first lady Prime Minister of the world.[9]

After the initial batch of students finished five years of Primary Education, classes had to be extended to provide Secondary Education and in due course classes up to Year 13 were established. Due to the patronage of former principals Miss. Wimala Liyanage (1973–1982), and Mrs R.M.L. Jayasekera (1982–2000) the status of the school was raised to level of a National School in 1991. Under the guidance of Miss W.P.N. De Silva (2000–2003) the school's academic and co-curricular activities were further developed.

Mrs P.M. Kalubowila assumed duties as the principal from 6 November 2003 having joined Sirimavo Bandaranaike Vidyalaya in 1986 as a Chemistry teacher. Ever since up to date Mrs Kalubowila also has been dedicated herself to serve the school in the sphere of educational and co-curricular activities and to upgrade the infra-structure facilities and resources development of the school.[10]

In July 2009, Mrs Kalubowila ordered all students to shut down their Facebook profiles, with a threat of expulsion from school for disobedience. This sparked a controversy in the school system in Sri Lanka. After the retirement of Mrs P.M. Kalubowila in February 2012, the newly appointed principal Mrs Dhammika C. Jayaneththi has taken over. Mrs Malini Herath was appointed as principal in 2013 and she is class 1 in Sri Lanka Education Administrative Service.

Southlands College, Galle

Southlands College, also known as Southlands Girls, is a **Girls' school** located in **Galle**, Sri Lanka founded in

1885 by the **Wesleyan Methodist** missionaries.

Southlands College is situated within the historical **Galle fort**.

Southlands College is the premier Girls school in Southern Sri Lanka. It was started during the British rule in 1885. Miss. Lucy Vanderstraaten was the first Principal. The school began in two larger down-stair rooms in a house in Fort with a group of some 50 children. It was originally named "Wesleyan Girls School".

Sri Parakramabahu Vidyalaya

St. Benedicts' College

St. Benedict's College is a Roman Catholic school located in Kotahena in Colombo 001500. The school was originally founded in 1838 at Wolfendhal (Colombo 13 East) by the Diocese of Ceylon as the Kottanchina Seminary. In 1868 it was renamed by the De La Salle Brothers as St. Benedict's College, beginning in 1868, making it the oldest Catholic school on the island, in existence for over 180 years.

St. Bridget's Convent

On 1 February 1902, at the request of T. A. Melizan, Archbishop of Colombo, St. Bridget's Convent was established as the second house of the Good Shepherd congregation for the education of young ladies. It was the third school in Colombo city, opened by the nuns. The first classes were held at a rented house on Turret Road in Colpetty, called 'The Firs' before moving to the present location, the premises of the former Henley House, Horton Place in 1912.Two sisters, Mary of St. Francis Borgia and Mary of Our lady of Lourdes, came from the original Kotahena Convent school (Good Shepherd Convent)) to undertake this work.

St. Claires College

St Clare's College started as a missinary school in 1899 but now it has changed the appearance into a government school with 104 teachers in both Tamil and Sinhala media under one Administrative principal. It is to stated proudly that now it has expanded into two sections as for Primary and Secondary with nearly 2000 children studying here with peace and harmony. This has become a gift to the multi-cultural community around Wellawatta area w

St. John's Girls School, Panadura

St. John's Girls' School was founded by Mrs Amelia Jansz in the year 1885 with the support of her husband Mr. Cyril Arnold Jansz who was the founder of St John's Schools and Colleges. The girls' school also came under the umbrella of the St John's Schools and Colleges. It is in

keeping with the idea that the girls' school should flourish even in the absence of the founders that Mr. Cyril Arnold Jansz appointed Board of Trustees to see to the total wellbeing of the girl's school. Thus, he gave sole ownership of the girl school to the Board of Trustees, comprising of one member from the Jansz family, three members from the Association of the Old Johnians and one member from the staff of the girls' school.

St. Josephs' College, Colombo

St. Joseph's College is, by popular acknowledgement, Sri Lanka's leading Roman Catholic School for boys. Effectively unchallenged, it has occupied this position ever since it was founded in 1896 by French missionaries led by Rev. Fr. Christophe-Etienne Bonjean.

Over the years, the College has seen many changes Like all enduring institutions, it has often been obliged to adapt to the needs and constraints of the historical movement. Yet, in spite of inevitable changes, St. Joseph's has never deviated from its principal goal of producing men of faith, knowledge and virtue whose loved ones, fellow workers and society at large may safely rely upon, and, from whose labour and advice they may continue to benefit as they have already done for well over a century.

St. Lawrences School

St. Lawrence's Convent is a Roman Catholic Girls' School, which is patronized by the congregation of Good shepherd nuns.

The school is known as a little oasis, which presented hundreds of valuable citizens to the nation in her unique history.

Providence works in unexpected ways. When Mrs Janet Poulier began her little drawing room school in the year 1900 in a house called Lawrence Villa. she never envisaged that in later years the city of Colombo would be dedicated to St. Lawrence, in whose name the first Catholic Church was built in the Fort of Colombo by Lorenzo De Almeida whose patron saint happened to be the same St Lawrence. When Fr. Robert Fernando built the new parish Church of Wellawatte, he dedicated it to this same Saint- the lover of poor and friend of the youth. Perhaps it was the name of her house that made Mrs Poulier interested in the life and work of St. Lawrence. Through a Protestant by denomination, in later years she called her school St. Lawrences School.

The Poulier School flourished under this great lady, an educationist dedicated to her calling. In 1930 when Mrs Janet Poulier found the pressure of work hard to handle, she appointed her niece Miss. Gladys Poulier her successor, though she still remained on the scene as consultant & adviser.

In the early year the school catered to both boys & girls. Mrs Poulier and her noble band of teachers worked tirelessly and school expanded moving premises. Lawrence villa which later became the old post office at the site of which stands todays structure, across the Galle Road, where Mrs Poulir purchased land for her new school building.

When she decided to sell the school, Mrs Poulier was adamant that the school should remain an educational institution and refusing an offer of Rs. 200,000 she accepted the Rs. 150,000 offer of Fr.Robert on condition that it remained a school and always bear the name of Lawrence. Thus in 1951 Fr. Robert Fernando purchased the school on behalf of the Catholic Church. The school came under the direction of Miss. Gozmao. In 1953 two Good Shepherd sisters with mother Finbarr as the head of the school began their work here. Certain changes were inevitable but the school continued along the same line for some years more.

Girls and boys continued to be educated here till later on the boys were allowed to remain only up till standard 5 and in the early sixties they were stop altogether. Sinhala, Tamil and English classes ran parallelly though numbers at the start were small. Some of the dilapidated classrooms gave way to a new building which included a laboratory as well. An old house at the bottom of the garden gave way to a two storeyed building.

One of the stalwarts from Mrs Pouliers time who continued to serve the school for many years afterwards on the administrative staff and gave her best loyal and devoted service to the school is the unforgettable Miss. Lou Bartholemeuz. She was associated with the school for almost half of its extince.

The school went onwards from strength to strength and today as an assisted private school holds its own as a small school producing well conducted all round students who take their place in the todays society holding responsible position in various fields. Ten principals have held office in the second half of the school existence with each principal developing the school in one field or the other.

Since it was initially a private school the staff was not transferred and many there were who spent their entire teaching career in the school. The success of the school was in large measure the result of their dedicated loyal services. A word about our parents who were always with the management at all times,- supporting , advising but never interfering in the administration of the school. The wonderful rapport between the management, parents and teachers is worthy of note as it contribute much to the development of the school.

The hallmark of a true Lawrentian is courtesy, versatility and responsibility. Small is beautiful they say- it is advantageous as well. Since the numbers are manageable there is more interaction between students and Teachers and among the students as well. The child, her skills and talents, her home background are all known and these help the teachers to bring out the best in a child or offer her guidance and support when necessary.

God has been generous with his gifts to St. Lawrences and has helped us to grow not just in age but in wisdom and grace as well. To him we humbly rededicate ourselves and declare that all we did was for The greater glory of God as our motto invites us to our patron St. Lawrence we add our salutations with the prayer that his inspiration and guidance will lead us ever onward to greater height and achievement.

St. Lucias College

St. Lucia's College (commonly known as St. Lucia's or Lucia's) is a Roman Catholic school located in Kotahena area of **Colombo, Sri Lanka**. This school was founded in 1880 and it is a Government School, managed by **Ministry of Education (Sri Lanka)**, which provides primary and secondary education.

The School Motto both "Pro Deo et Patria" written in Latin phrase and "मेरा देवाय स स्वदेशाय।" (Swa devvaya sa swadeshaaya) written in Sanskrit phrase having same meaning as "For God and Country".

St. Pauls' Milagiriya

The school was founded on 14 January 1887 as a Parish School attached to the St. Paul's Church of Milagiriya with only 24 students and 4 teachers.

The first principal of the school was Mrs Stella Coban. In the early years of the legendary pathway of the school the majority of the students belonged to the Burger community and the medium of education was English. Later until 1957 the School had given education in all Sinhala, Tamil and English medium.

Throughout the history, St.Paul's has accordingly endowed the nation with a generation of accomplished ladies including medical,engineering, law, science and arts graduates and professionals in every field. With the glorious history of 131 years the school has expanded its capacities in every aspect. Today it nourishes the souls of more than 4,500 students with the help of an academic staff of 150 and a non-academic Staff of 25.

St. Peters' College

St. Peter's College, a recognized hallmark of education was established on 18 January 1922 by Rev. Fr. Maurice Le Goc. With the dawn of 2021, St. Peter's College is only 12 months away from celebrating its centenary. Guided by many visionary Rectors for nearly ten decades, St. Peter's College has braved many a storm and risen to be one of the leading Educational Institutions in Sri Lanka. Catering to the demands of present generation, St. Peter's is now known among educationists as an excellent seat of learning.

St. Sebastian's Balika Maha Vidyalaya, Kandana

St. Thomas' College

S.Thomas' College Mount Lavinia is a premier Anglican Church boys School, in greater Colombo founded on Feb 3 1851, by the First Bishop of Ceylon Rt. Rev. James Chapman DD, whose vision was to build a College and Cathedral for his new Diocese. Thus on the 3rd of February 1851 the College of St. Thomas the Apostle, Colombo was opened with the objectives of training

Christian Clergy and making its sons good citizens through the discipline and supervision of the Christian Faith.

Although Christian values were the corner stone on which the School was founded, students of all races, ethnicities, castes, social classes and religions studied together in harmony. Despite his hopes that the School would be a cradle for local ordained ministry Bishop Chapman himself lamented that he recognized that it had become more secular and pluralistic in its outlook than he would have wished and he expressed concern about need to maintain the Christian character of the School. This has been done. Today S. Thomas' College is very much a Christian and Anglican institution in that it maintains the fundamental tenets of the Christian Faith within the Anglican ethos of comprehensiveness and inclusivity.

The School grew from strength to strength in Mutwal, for over three score years, carefully nurtured by several dedicated educators who served as Warden (the title for Headmaster deliberately chosen by Bishop Chapman), among them, the Rev'd Dr C. W. Wood (1st Warden), the Ven. E. F.Miller (who also served as Archdeacon of Colombo), the Rev'd W. A. Buck and the Rev'd W. A. Stone. By 1916, Warden Stone, found that the environs of Mutwal that had become adversely affected by coal dust from the Colombo Harbour when coal powered ships replaced ships with sails, were not best suited for his pupils and so with the support and blessings of Bishop E. A. Copleton and Mr C. E. A Dias, embarked on an ambitious plan to shift the School from Mutwal to Mount Lavinia. It is significant that Mount Lavinia had been Bishop Chapman's first choice as a location for his School when he had been looking for a suitable location in 1849. But the cost of purchasing the house that was once the Governor's Residence and later the Mount Lavinia Grand Hotel was considered prohibitive at that time and he had abandoned the idea. The School reopened at the new site in Mount Lavinia on the 26th of January 1918 under Warden Stone's courageous leadership. Since then a number of great Wardens, among them the Ven. K. C. McPherson (later Archdeacon of Bombay), the Rev'd Canon R. S. de Saram (the first old boy of the School and son of the soil to be Warden as well as the longest serving, retiring in 1958 after 26 years in office), Mr. C. H. L. Davidson (the first layman to be Warden) and Mr W. M. N de Alwis have ensured that the vision and core values (traditions), handed down from generation to generation were maintained untarnished and unimpaired. In 1951 under Warden de Saram's courageous leadership S. Thomas' College became a full private and fee levying but government approved School.

The College has been managed since 1927 by a representative Board of Governors chaired by the Anglican Bishop of Colombo who is also known by his historic title as the 'Visitor to the College'. The administration and day to day management of the College itself is headed by a Warden assisted by a Sub Warden.

There is also a School Chaplaincy connected with the famous Chapel of the Transfiguration.

The School is divided into the Primary or Lower School (with Grades 1 – 5 known by their traditional names of Kindergarten, Form I, Form II, Lower III and Upper III), Lower Secondary or Middle School (with Grades 6 – 9 known by their traditional names of Lower IV, Upper IV,

Form V & Lower VI) and Upper Secondary or Upper School (with Grades 10 and 11) and thereafter divided into three main Senior School Advanced Level sections (known as the College Forms B, A & E) for Arts and Commerce, Science and the International of London Advanced Levels. Each of the Sections is headed by a Head of Section under whom there are Deputy Heads, Sectional Heads and Faculty Heads for each subject group. The sections were restructured in 2017.

A Nursery School was opened for the sons and daughters of Old Boys and Staff in January 2017, allowing students from as young as 2+ to enter this School. The boys students passing out from the Nursery gain entry into Kindergarten automatically while the girls seek admission to one of our corresponding schools for girls in Colombo.
S. Thomas' College is widely reputed to have one of the most beautiful school campuses in Sri Lanka, approximately half an hour's drive from the southern limits of the City of Colombo. The entrance to the school is marked by the awe-inspiring Chapel of the Transfiguration, which towers over the rest of the campus. The Chapel is a vital element in the education at STC and is the centre of the spiritual life of the College, where the spirituality of many generations of Thomians have been formed and most importantly experienced God over the years. Synonymous with the Chapel is it's world famous Choir that made its debut in 1854 as the Choir of the new Cathedral of Christ in Colombo that was consecrated in the precincts of the School at Mutwal that year. Dominating the interior of this Byzantine structure from the apse in David Paynter's masterpiece mural depicting the Transfiguration of Jesus that was completed and dedicated in 1968 with its unique image of a beardless Christ. Dear

to the hearts of all Thomians of diverse faiths and races, the Chapel serves as a reminder to us of our heritage, which is a gift of God.

Connected with the School Chapel is the Chaplaincy served by a full-time Chaplain and a Chaplaincy Team. The Chaplain leads a team of full-time School Counsellors and also coordinates the Sound Mind Sound Body Programme which is a unique programme for S. Thomas' College.

Beyond the famous Quadrangle, the main school buildings, the College Hall, the Dormitories and Library, the vast campus, modeled on the traditional English public school, stretches down to the famous golden beaches of Mount Lavinia, reaching the deep blue Indian Ocean.
S. Thomas' provides a sound education in both Local (G. C. E. A/L & O/L) & London A/L Examination systems. Instructions are given in Sinhala and Tamil in the Lower School, and in all three media from the Middle School to the College Forms (A/L).

The biggest asset possessed by the School is the student body which presently comprises of about 2800 members of varied faiths and ethnicities. It is a well-disciplined community and excels in both academic and extra and co-curricular activities.

S. Thomas' was the first school in Sri Lanka to have its own swimming pool, gifted the School in 1933 by Dr. R. L. Hayman (later Sub Warden and also founding Headmaster of S. Thomas' College at Gurutalawa in 1942). The Big Club and the Small Club grounds afford Thomians the facilities for many sports; namely Cricket,

Rugby, Soccer, Athletics and Hockey. There are also well-laid courts for Tennis and Basketball. In 1994 the Indoor Cricket Nets were added and the pinnacle of all facilities the Indoor Sports Complex in 3 phases was completed in 1996. The sports complex houses Table Tennis facilities, several Badminton Courts, 3 glass backed Squash courts – all to international standards, together with a well equipped Gymnasium.

The annual Cricket Encounter between S. Thomas' College and Royal College (known as the Big Match or the Battle of the Blues) is the second oldest uninterrupted cricket encounter in the world, the first being the inter-collegiate match between St Peter's College and Prince Alfred College I Adelaide, Australia that commenced one year before the Royal-Thomian in 1878.

S. Thomas' also boasts of more than 50 student Societies and Clubs. The Student Christian Movement and the other 3 religious societies play an important role in fostering religious educationand nurturing the spirituality of the Thomian youth. The Chapel Choir still continues to maintain the highest standards in Anglican Choral Music and is perhaps one of the only school choirs in Asia to be affiliated to the Royal School of Church Music in the United Kingdom. The annual Festal Service of Nine Lessons and Carols which was initiated by the Revd. Canon Roy Yin in 1946 is an eagerly awaited event and is modelled on that of Kings' College, Cambridge where Fr Yin had served as an Assistant Chaplain prior to coming to Sri Lanka as Chaplain of STC. The Guild of All Souls for Altar Servers also plays a vital role in the Chapel and the servers assist the Chaplain at Chapel Services. The other Clubs and Societies offer a range of activities and involvements from the educational to social welfare. The Thomian Union, the English Literary and Debating Society (the oldest Society of the School), the English Drama society, the Science Associations, the Commerce Society, the Interact Club, the UN Club, the ICT Club and the Culinary Arts Society are some of them. Among other activities, STC has the various Bands, Scouting and Cadeting and a College Magazine that has been published since 1875.

The School runs a Boarding, which since the inception of the College, has provided many Thomians from distant regions of Sri Lanka a *'home away from home'*.

S. Thomas' has over the years produced many Thomians who have rendered great service to their Church, to the Nation and to whichever country in the world where many of them have migrated.

STC has made a significant contribution to Sri Lanka's progress. Among its proud products stand a host of Christian Clergymen, Statesmen (including Prime Ministers the Rt. Hon. D. S. Senanayake, the Hon. Dudley Senanayake, the Hon. S. W. R. D Bandaranaike and the Hon. W. Dahanayaka), Cabinet Ministers, Members of the Judiciary, Scholars, Scientists, Diplomats, Doctors, Engineers, Accountants, Musicians, Artists, Dramatists.

S. Thomas' College is therefore much more than just a school. It is an institution rich in tradition, characterized by almost 175 years of hard work, dedication and achievement, all imbibed with the legendary Thomian Spirit. It has been a pioneering institution which has understood and nurtured the very best in youth; where mere boys came in and great men went out to be *"men and gentlemen always"*, men who beat the odds with the legendary Thomian grit and gentlemen who have always upheld the motto of the School given to it by the Founder himself – "Esto Perpetua", Be Thou Forever.

Thurstan College

Founded in 1950, Thurstan College is one of the leading schools in the country with a student population of approximately 2500. It is situated in Colombo 7, in the heart of the educational triangle of Sri Lanka with University of Colombo & Royal College being the neighbors. The College has made giant strides after its humble beginning.

Thurstan College has been blessed over the years with dedicated staff who have become more than teachers to their young students. This has resulted in students achieving academic success in the examinations conducted by the Education Ministry in Sri Lanka and proceeding to Universities and Higher Educational Institutes in Sri Lanka and Overseas. The facilities at College range from modern Science laboratory facilities, Computer laboratories to libraries, which are equipped with the most recent publications of books, journals and periodicals.

College is well known not only for its high academic standards but also, for their achievements in Sports and excellence in Extra Curricular Activities. The College has more than 30 clubs and societies, which gives students an opportunity to gain knowledge in various disciplines and also show their hidden talents and skills at public forum. They also give an opportunity for students to show their leadership capabilities. Thurstan is well known for it's achievements for sports and has a Junior & a Senior play ground, a Swimming pool, tennis courts and other sports facilities for students. The College believes in producing all round students, well trained to overcome the trails & tribulations at the world at large. Some of the sports played are Cricket, Rugby, Tennis, Table Tennis Badminton and Chess.

Rich in traditions and equipped with all the modern facilities needed for a College, Thurstan is no doubt one of the best Colleges in the island.

Rev. Richard Collins founded Trinity College (as The Kandy Collegiate School) in 1872, under the auspices of the Christian Missionary Society based on the traditions of public schools in England. The missionaries took into their ambit the best of our indigenous culture. Today it is one of the leading schools in the country and boasts a rich heritage. The grand Principal of Trinity College Rev. A.G.

Fraser brought the school from being a mere provincial school to the status of a national college. In his day (1904-1924) and decades to follow, it became a multi faceted educational institution, equal to that of any leading school in the British Commonwealth. In fact it went beyond being National as in that era boys came to Trinity just to receive their education from countries such as Burma, some African countries, Maldives and Southern India.

Although Trinity College was founded in 1872, its antecedents go back to 1818 when the first missionaries from Britain penetrated the Kandyan Kingdom. Rev. and Mrs Thomas Browning set up a Mission House in this location, despite the anti-British rebellion that had just shaken the country then known as Ceylon. It was in this Mission House in 1823 that Rev Ireland Jones started an Elementary School of humble proportions which after it closed twice was re established in 1872 by Rev Richard Collins.

Trinity's mission is to provide the best all-round education for the boys in a caring, disciplined and inspiring environment. This includes academic studies, sports, the Arts and extra-curricular activities.

True to the principles of its Anglican founders, Trinity College has always endeavoured to instill and nurture qualities such as respect, compassion, self-discipline, fairness, honesty and integrity. As an Anglican school, but with children from many different religions, we believe that these virtues are valued not only by Christians, but by members of all faiths.

Trinity College aims to produce the next generation of leaders in Sri Lanka. As such, boys should leave the school confident, articulate, well-balanced and able to think for themselves. They should be comfortable both in English and in their mother tongue. They should be ambitious and determined, yet sensitive to the needs of others. And they should be critical and creative thinkers, who are ready to make a positive difference to their country and to the world.

Trinity College has around 3,000 pupils. Starting at the age of 3 at Montessori Nursery, gives very young children their initial experience of school. The Junior School discovers and nurtures a child's unique talents and strengths; it gives opportunities for boys to try out new and exciting activities; and it provides a sound academic foundation to take to the next level. The Middle School aims to create hard-working, creative, active and disciplined students, who are encouraged to think for themselves. Academic study is balanced by a wide variety of sports and extra-curricular activities. And the Upper School provides multiple academic and extra-curricular opportunities within a stimulating environment; thereby enabling our boys to develop the life-skills to become leaders at all levels of society.

Uduppidy American Misson College

Was founded on 4 January 1852 by the American Ceylon
Mission

Veluwana College

Veluwana College, in **Dematagoda** was established on 11 Jun 1951 by the **Buddhist** Society, led by the Veluwanarama Temple. It is one of oldest Buddhist schools in **Sri Lanka**. Veluwana College is a National School. It provides **primary** and **secondary education**.

Visakha Vidyalaya

Visakha Vidyalaya was founded on the 16th of January, 1917 by the late Mrs Jeremias Dias as an institution of learning for the Buddhist girls of this land at a time when such institutions were rare.

Begun under the name of "Buddhist Girls' College" in a house called "The Firs" at Turret Road, Colombo, it was moved to its present premises at Vajira Road on the 21st of November 1927 and named "Visakha Vidyalaya" by Lady Stanley, the wife of the then Governor of Ceylon. From humble beginnings, it has risen to the position of the most sought after school for girls in Sri Lanka, and the only girls' school to be identified amongst the first National Schools in the Island.

Starting with just 20 students way back in 1917, she has about 4,000 students on her roll today, with an academic staff numbering 146. Today, Visakha stands unchallenged. It is at the top of all the schools in the Island for academic excellence and the prestige she enjoys is indeed a fitting tribute to her founder. Her records in sports and other co curricular activities are no less worthy of mention. Indeed, the most remarkable characteristic of Visakha is her ability to blend the best of the traditional and the modern aspects of life. An Old Girl is found leading the way in every field; be it academic, professional or aesthetics giving credence to the fact that the proudly uttered words "I am a Visakhian" mean so much.

The school owes its origin to the far-sightedness and philanthropy of her noble Founder, its development to the vision and leadership of the long line of Managers and Principals and its continued standard of excellence to the devotion and loyalty of its Teachers, Parents and Students, both past and present.

Vivekananda College

Vivekananda College, founded in 1926 during British Colonial rule, was the first Hindu school that was set up in Colombo to uplift education in the island.

It was setup thanks to the efforts of Swami Vipulanandar and Swami Sachithanandan on March 24, 1926, and drew its inspiration from the historic visit to the island by Indian spiritual leader, Swami Vivekananda in 1897.

The school's first Principal was K. Arunachalam and the first manager was Arunachalam Mahadeva

Swami Vivekananda's views on education can be encapsulated by the dictum, 'become a good human being - make a good human being'. The motto of the school ("Be and Make") drew from this thought while the school song, authored by Ponnambalam speaks of bringing together energy, education and wisdom.

The school admitted both girls and boys from its inception. In 1953 and 1963 the school began preparing students for the O/L and A/L exams. In 1967, the school was able to produce its first university entrant.

All this happened at a time when the school was relatively impoverished in terms of physical facilities. The lack of classrooms was a major problem. However, undeterred by this, the students and teachers decided to have classes in the evenings as well to circumvent this problem.

The evening classes which commenced in 1954, were an integral part of the educational programme until very recently.

In recent years problems such as the lack of electricity and buildings were resolved. However, it is interesting that the school recorded what is widely held as its Golden Age (1972 to 1983) amidst these problems.

That was the time of Principal Maheshan. He dedicated himself to the development of the school. He worked tirelessly, day and night, and also obtained the help of people in the neighbourhood, even going on house-to-house campaigns.

Wesley College: DOUBLE BLUE

Wesley College is named after John Wesley (1703-1791), the founder of the Methodist Church. An Oxford graduate, he was one of the greatest evangelists in the history of the Christian Church. A preacher of great power and an organizer of genius, he founded Methodism in the face of intense opposition and laid the foundations of future world-wide expansion.

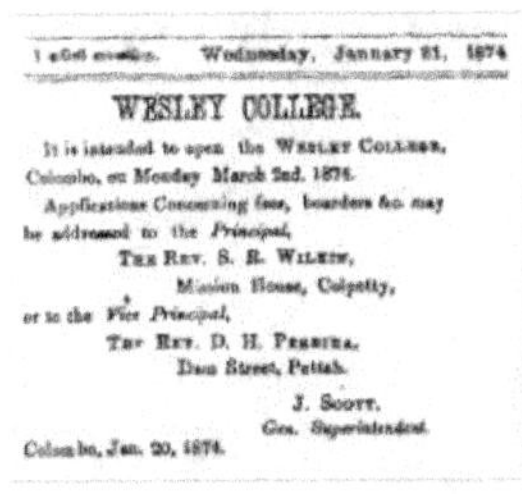

Wesley College began its life in Dam Street Pettah and was founded by Rev. Daniel Henry Pereira on the 2nd of March 1874. He became its first Vice Principal during the Principalship of Rev. Samuel Rowse Wilkin. Dam Street takes us back to the Dutch period. During the early days

Pettah was a respectable residential area and its streets were lined by tall trees. Messenger Street was called 'Rue de Massang' by the Dutch as there were many Massang trees. Even today it is called Massang Gas Vidiya. Earlier Dam Street was called 'Damba Street' as Damba trees lined its path. The school had its beginnings on the dusty verandahs of the old Methodist Church at Dam Street, Pettah. Following is a notice published in the Weekly Christian Journal- Satyalankaraya or The Beauty of Truth on the 21st of January 1874.

Closely associated with Rev Pereira was Jan Crozier, a kindly Boer from the South African Rand. The Pettah merchants of mixed race and religions sent their children to receive their education in this school.

Daniel Henry Pereira was much loved by the people and his pupils. He laboured thus for years in the dust and the heat of Pettah. When Rev Highfield arrived In 1895 Pettah was rapidly becoming industrialized and he saw the need for quieter surroundings for his school with room to expand. Wesley College was moved to its present site in 1905 with the help of the dynamic Rev. Henry Highfield.

Reminiscences of Wesley in Pettah by Henry Highfield

I was one of four young Missionaries who left London in the British India "Golconda" for the East in September 1895. Two went on further for India. R.C. Oliver and I were for Ceylon and so left the ship at Colombo in the early hours of a mid-October day, being met by Rev. T. Moscrop and Mr. S. Passmore.

Mr. Passmore was to initiate me into the work of Wesley College and Mr. Moscrop was Chairman of the Colombo District and a former Principal of Wesley. I lived with him and Mrs Moscrop until they left to return into the work at home. I was thus exceptionally fortunate in having two such fine and experienced men to guide me at the start.
Besides this, when Mr. Passmore took me the next day to Wesley I quickly found that I had two other unusually fine and experienced men on the Staff. Charles Peter Dias joined Wesley in its second year (1876) and continued as Head Master until after my departure in 1925. So too did W.E. Mack, the first assistant; and both, but especially Mr. Dias were of the very greatest help, not at the start only but all along, and the School should never forget what it owes to them. Of the premises I had a very different opinion and I think from the very first I was resolved that the School must have a better habitation.

It was good for Wesley that she had in Dias a genuine Church of England Christian and in Mack a good representative of the Dutch Reformed Faith. I quickly realised that the school believed in itself and was on its toes to spring forward towards the front and in Redlich and Honter we had two who would give any other school a hard tussle for the first place in scholarship.

Before Mr. Passmore took charge Mr. Hillard, venturing boldly, had built the one building that had given the School an Assembly Hall in which all could gather together twice a day and so get to feel their corporate existence. This hall too served for the teaching of four large classes – not an ideal state of things. It is true that Hillard was unable to get it paid for but he wisely pledged the future to make good. So when in 1899 Wesleyan Methodism at Home set out to raise a million guineas from a million Methodists and successfully reached the target, as we would call it, the resolve in my heart on the first day of my seeing the school was confirmed. As however none of these guineas was to be spent in cancelling debts I had to become a beggar. It was done almost as in a dream during the last six months of 1899, and so eventually the Committee at Home gave me a promise of five times all that we could raise in Ceylon.

By the end of 1904 that came to Rs.35,000 and the Committee, though much surprised by the total, stood to their promise and the building facing Base Line Road was erected and opened early in 1907 with the Director of Education, John Harward (previously Principal of Royal College), as chief speaker.

The Rev. Daniel Henry Perera - Founder of Wesley College, Colombo

In a Journey; back in time; to the environs of the dusty noisy Pettah, we go over to the Wesleyan Mission premises in Dam Street, where we find a group of children at the feet of a benign Minister, the Rev. Daniel Henry Pereira. It certainly was no place for a school but in spite of the many difficulties, no doubt inspired by the Lord's invitation "suffer the little children to come unto me" this man kept his grace. Rev. Daniel Henry Pereira, born (circa) 1926 was the eldest son of the Rev. Don Daniel Pereira, who started life as a young school master and taught in a school built by the Rev. Benjamin Clough. On joining the Ministry he followed deep evangelistic trends. He was called "the apostle of Kurana – Negombo ". The Rev. Daniel Henry Pereira had a younger brother, who was Rev. Peter Bartholomeusz Pereira.

Young Daniel Henry was keenly interested in teaching and at a very early age took an equally great interest in the snakes which he studied identifying their species and habits under a famous South Indian Snake Specialist who reserved no secrets as he instructed his pupil. Daniel Henry was quick to absorb the life pattern of these ophidian reptiles. In fact, in later years, he had edited a catalogue in Sinhala and had contributed to journals. He submitted papers to the Ceylon Friend a journal associated with the Wesleyan Church. His contribution to these many journals gave rise to research. He was also an authority on ants in Ceylon.

He had great hopes of being a scientist, but in response to his dying mother's wish he entered the Ministry in 1851. In addition to his knowledge of reptiles, ants, snails and slugs as a nature scientist he was also proficient in English, Sinhala and Portuguese. His fluency and masterly use of these languages kept his congregation spellbound. He had also knowledge of Hebrew and Greek. He had a brilliant mind displaying itself in his clarity of expression. Certainly he would have been on par with the Western Missionaries of evangelistic fervour. He was a pupil of the famed Oriental Scholar, the Rev. Don John Gogerley who was in charge of the Institute of Colombo, which was an early "Divinity School". His interest in teaching, combined with his parish work and his deep interest in natural science, made him eminent. In his Parish work he served in many stations for over 25 years. Moratuwa, then a very large Parish which he took over from the Rev. G. G. de Zilva, saw him work with zest and vigour. He founded an English School at Gorakagaha in Mankada, conducting cottage meetings in the homes of those Methodists whilst he resided at Rawattawatte. He contributed largely to the spiritual revival at Moratuwa. When he fell ill his work was taken over by the Rev. Robert Hardy. The school at Dam Street marked the beginning of Wesley College which was founded on the 2nd March 1874 of which he was the first ever Vice Principal, with the Rev. Samuel Rowse Wilkin its first Principal (from 1874 -1879) followed by the Rev. Arthur Shipham (1880 – 1883), with whom Rev. Daniel Henry Pereira worked till the latter's retirement. The Rev. Daniel Henry Pereira's son, William H. D. Pereira, studied at Wesley. He was later an Assistant Accountant in the Colombo Port Commission. On his retirement as a Minister in 1882 Rev Daniel Henry Pereira settled in Hambantota. Though not in the best of health, he visited homes of those persons who had surrendered their lives to Christ. They were greatly helped by this erudite but simple priest with his life style, though plain, rich in the -scriptures and its application. His was a life of deep prayer and faith of wide labour and concern, ever with an alert mind. His old friend Rev. Arthur Shipham who was stationed at Matara, no doubt may have had communication with each other. The last few months of his life had been a challenge. His health was failing but his discipline and training and his deep reliance on his Saviour had increased his faith. He faced the storm, yet on an even keel, though confined to his home with restricted movement.

A large number of villagers visited him. It was on the 22nd November 1886 that death took him. His was a life that laboured and was well spent in the Lord's vineyard as answering the Master's call "come follow me".

Wesley commemorates the memory of her Founder, the Rev. Daniel Henry Pereira, annually on Founder's Day – March 2nd. This is the most important event in the School's calendar. A three-storied imposing building dedicated to his memory, the "D. H. Pereira Memorial Building", built to accommodate the junior school, was constructed during the Principalship of Dunstan Fernando. No doubt the labours of the Rev. Daniel Henry Perera, servant of God, has nurtured a rich crop of which we in this present age are beneficiaries; no doubt this harvest will be reaped by generations yet unborn.

Rev. Henry Highfield

Henry Highfield is to Wesley what Thesius is to Greece. His legend is everywhere. Spurred on by his Missionary zeal and love for humanity he collected the money to build the school in its present site.

In the new Wesley there was pride in teaching and dignity in learning in an atmosphere of tranquillity and understanding.

On leaving school, boys were able to face the struggles of the wider world with courage and fortitude. He was born in Bengal, India in 1865, and was the son of Rev. George Henry Highfeld, who spent many years on the Indian mission-field. His early education was at Kingswood, England, and he afterwards took the MA degree at London and Cambridge. He was accepted as a candidate for the ministry, and after training at Richmond near London was sent to Ceylon in 1895. Here he had charge of Wesley College. Colombo, and remained in Ceylon for thirty years. On returning to England he served in the following circuits: Aberystwyth, Marazion and Cradley Heath. He retired to Pickering in 1936 and to within a few months of his death was actively engaged in the life of the circuit, taking regular preaching appointments and leading a society class.

He will always be remembered for his outstanding work in Ceylon. It was under his guidance that the new Wesley College at Colombo was built, at a cost of £15,000, and largely through his unremitting efforts this magnificent structure was opened free of debt. He cycled throughout the length and breadth of Ceylon soliciting subscriptions for the enterprise, and actually collected £2,500 in this way. He left a lasting impression on the public life of Ceylon and many of his former pupils came to occupy posts of great administrative responsibility. The first Governor-General of Ceylon was one of his old students. The Education Officer for Ceylon writes: Like "Arnold of Rugby ", he will ever be remembered as "Highfield of Wesley ". He excelled as an expository preacher, his intimate knowledge of New Testament Greek enabling him to present ever-fresh aspects of Christian truth. During his retirement he freely placed his knowledge at the disposal of the probationers in the Ryedale area and guided their studies. He exercised a wonderfully helpful ministry in the homes of his people, where he was ever a welcome visitor. He was utterly consecrated to his Lord and counted no sacrifice too great for the extension of the Kingdom. He was most generous in his financial support of the work of God at home and overseas, and never refused a duty he was able to fulfil. He died at Scarborough on 1st February 1955 in the ninetieth year of his life and in the sixtieth of his ministry. Henry Highfield is no more but his legend lives on.

The present site on which Wesley College stands and the surrounding land was once owned by Charles Ambrose Lorensz. The Burgher intelligentsia in the 1860s was led by a young man who hailed from Matara – Charles Ambrose Lorensz.

Being a brilliant lawyer he was popularly known as the "morning star of Hulftsdorf".

Together with a group of young Burghers like Leopold

Charles Ambrose Lorenz

Ludovici, Francis Bevan, Samuel Grenier and James Stewart Drieberg they produced a leading local literary journal called Young Ceylon.

In 1859 Lorensz and a syndicate purchased the Ceylon Examiner which became the first Ceylonese newspaper. Until his death in 1871, at the age of forty two, Lorensz wielded the powerful influence of his pen for social reform, championing democratic causes and courageously criticising the British colonial government, the Governor and his Executive Council. The Principal's bungalow was built around 1860. The architecture of the building is typical for that period with tall cylindrical columns supporting a large porch, a wide verandah and the lovely lounge with many spacious rooms. Part of the beautiful front garden has been taken over for the Chapel, a useful addition.

Yasodara Balika Vidyalaya

Yasodara Balika Vidyalaya (YBV), Colombo 8 has a glowing history as the first girls' school to be inaugurated in old Ceylon (Sri Lanka now) on July 20, 1846. The school marked in history as a Baptist Girls' College in the year 2014, which marked a milestone of the colleges 167 year of existence.

In 1846 the Baptist Missionary Society of England initiated this school as Baptist Girls' College with only 12 girls. During the early stages, former principals Ms. Boucher, Mrs Fergus, Mrs Evans and Mrs Gad made huge contributions to uplift the standard of the school.

Zahira College

Zahira College, Colombo was founded in 1892 as Al Madrasathul Zahira by two of the most prominent Sri Lankan Muslims of the day, I. L. M. Abdul Aziz and Arasi Marikar Wapchie Marikar, with the active patronage of Ahmed Orabi Pasha of Egypt.

It is currently the largest Muslim educational institution in

Sri Lanka with more than 5000 students studying there. The college is situated at the heart of Colombo city. The college also has one of the oldest mosques in the country in its premises.

Speech made by Mr. **S.L.M. Shafi Marikkar** (former Princiapl) at the Centenary Celebration of the college on 29th September, 1992.

The history of Muslim education culminating in the establishment of Zahira College is a fascinating study of the triumph of the human mind over environment and circumstance. Conceived by visionaries at a time when circumstances were positively hostile to English education, Muslim education succeeded in over-coming the constraints of an environment where English education was closely associated with proselytism that the elders of the community preferred lack of formal English education to the realities of an almost state aided conversion that had almost submerged other communities. Nevertheless our pioneers in education were more than satisfied that Islam would weather assaults at conversion but that education was essential for the community's progress if not its very survival. Thus did Zahira make its first faltering steps – not through state patronage, not through ministrations of foreign missionaries but through the vision of a few leaders whose enthusiasm by and by warmed an entire community to action.

The historic speech made by M. C. Siddhi Lebbe in 1891 in the Maradana Mosque Hall and his impassioned appeal to the Muslims to unite and promote the educational advancement of the community led to the formation of the Colombo Muslim Educational Society with I. L. M. Abdul Aziz as Secretary and A. M. Wappitchi Marikar as Treasurer. With the active patronage of Ahamed Orabi Pasha, the Egyptian exile in Ceylon the long cherished dream of the visionary M. C. Siddhi Lebbe became a reality when Al-Madrasathul Zahira was established on Monday 22nd of August 1892 with Wappitchi Marikar as its first Manage. In 1894 the school was registered as a grant-in-aid school Maradana Mohammedan Boys School – the number of pupils being 35.

In 1905 the foundation stone for a two-storied building was laid by **Moulavi Rafiudeen Ahmed** of Bombay who was in the island in connection with the Fez question. The building declared open by Ahmed Orabi Pasha in 1906. In 1911 the school was upgraded as a Secondary School and in 1913 re-named Muslim Zahira College – Mr. O. E. Martinus, BA as its first Principal.
In 1917 Wappitchi Marikar handed over the management of the College to the Maradana Mosque after having successfully managed the school for twenty-five years. Mr. N. H. M. Abdul Cader, Proctor SC took over as Manager in 1917. In 1919 Mr. A. S. Abdul Cader, the first Muslim Trained teacher was appointed Headmaster.

Although Zahira College was now established on strong foundation yet it was apparent that he enthusiasm and optimism of the early pioneers was somewhat waning leading even to the reduction of the number of pupils from the earlier figure of 108 in 1909.

It was at this stage that the Maradana Muslim Committee

through its Manager N. H. M. Abdul Cader invited Mr. T. B. Jayah to take up the Principalship of the College.

Zahira is derived from the Arabic word "Zahir", which means "Evident" or "Visible".

About the Compiler

Fazli Sameer was born, on 16 February, 1948, in Bambalapitiya, Colombo-4, and was educated in the English Medium at Royal Primary School (1953-58) and Royal College (1959-66), Colombo. In 1967/68 he spent the first year of the course in BSc. Physical Science at the University of Colombo and left thereafter to pursue a course in Computer Science with IBM.

His employment covered stints at Chartered Bank in Colombo (1979-89), Citibank in the Middle East (1979-1999), Al Faisaliah Group in Saudi Arabia (1999-2008) in Information Technology, and private Business & IT Consulting from 2008 to date.

Since 1979, Fazli has been engaged in researching, collecting, and publishing Sri Lanka genealogy of all Sri Lankan communities. He published, Family Tree Data: Genealogical Tables of Sri Lankan Muslims in 1996, and manages the SriLanka Genealogy Website on the internet at http://www.worldgenweb.org/lkawgw

Fazli has also been researching, preserving and publishing the history and legacy of Sri Lankan people, places, and significant events. He writes and manages a blog, titled F's Place which contains valuable data of streets, people, homes, and families who lived in Colombo in the 1960s:

http://kermeey.blogspot.com He is also into prose and poetry on his personal blog. F's Space: http://kermeey2.blogspot.com

His other works include, February Frolic (a book of verse), collected volumes of Ceylon Moor, Burgher, Sinhalese, & Tamil Family Trees, Wellawatte Ways, Kaleidoscopic Kollupitiya, The Way We Were (an autobiography), Sophie Akka & Somapala (cartoons), Ceylon Moor Families of Turkish origin, Jonathan Livingstone Kabaragoya. He contributes to the English Writers Workshop in Colombo since January 2019.

Fazli married Shirani Ibrahim in 1974. They have two daughters, Melina & Nadia and two grandkids, Maria & Abdullah.

Reading and writing was always a great passion in the Sameer household in Bambalapitiya, in Colombo. Newspapers, magazines, and books were freely available, in abundance, for everyone to indulge in.